FAN CLUB

I Love KRISTEN STEWART

Kat Miller

WINDMILL
BOOKS

New York

Published in 2011 by Windmill Books, LLC
303 Park Avenue South, Suite # 1280, New York, NY 10010-3657

CREDITS:
Editor: Jennifer Way
Book Design: Erica Clendening and Greg Tucker
Photo Research: Ashley Burrell

Photo Credits: Cover, p. 22 Gabriel Bouys/AFP/Getty Images; cover background, pp. 5, 6–7, 9, 13 (top), 17 (top), 18–19 Shutterstock.com; p. 4 Barry King/FilmMagic/Getty Images; p. 7 Gregg DeGuire/WireImage/Getty Images; pp. 8–9 Vera Anderson/WireImage/Getty Images; p. 11 Franco S. Origlia/Getty Images; pp. 12–13 Kevin Mazur/WireImage/Getty Images; p. 15 Lester Cohen/WireImage/Getty Images; p. 16 (top) Todd Williamson/WireImage/Getty Images; pp. 16–17 C Flanigan/FilmMagic/Getty Images; p. 19 (top) Jason LaVeris/FilmMagic/Getty Images; pp. 20–21 James Devaney/WireImage/Getty Images.

Library of Congress Cataloging-in-Publication Data

Miller, Kat.
 I love Kristen Stewart / by Kat Miller.
    p. cm. — (Fan club)
 Includes index.
 ISBN 978-1-61533-060-7 (library binding) — ISBN 978-1-61533-061-4 (pbk.) — ISBN 978-1-61533-062-1 (6-pack)
 1. Stewart, Kristen, 1990– —Juvenile literature. 2. Actors—United States—Biography—Juvenile literature. I. Title.
 PN2287.S685M55 2011
 791.4302'8092—dc22
 [B]

                                    2010008388

Manufactured in the United States of America

For more great fiction and nonfiction, go to windmillbooks.com.

CPSIA Compliance Information: Batch #S10W: For further information contact Windmill Books, New York, New York at 1-866-478-0556.

Contents

Meet Kristen Stewart

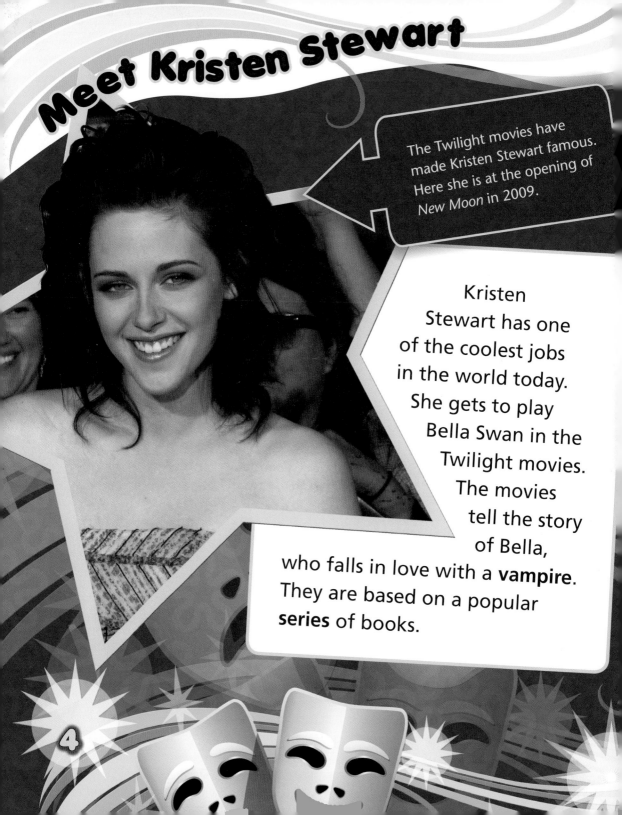

The Twilight movies have made Kristen Stewart famous. Here she is at the opening of *New Moon* in 2009.

Kristen Stewart has one of the coolest jobs in the world today. She gets to play Bella Swan in the Twilight movies. The movies tell the story of Bella, who falls in love with a **vampire**. They are based on a popular **series** of books.

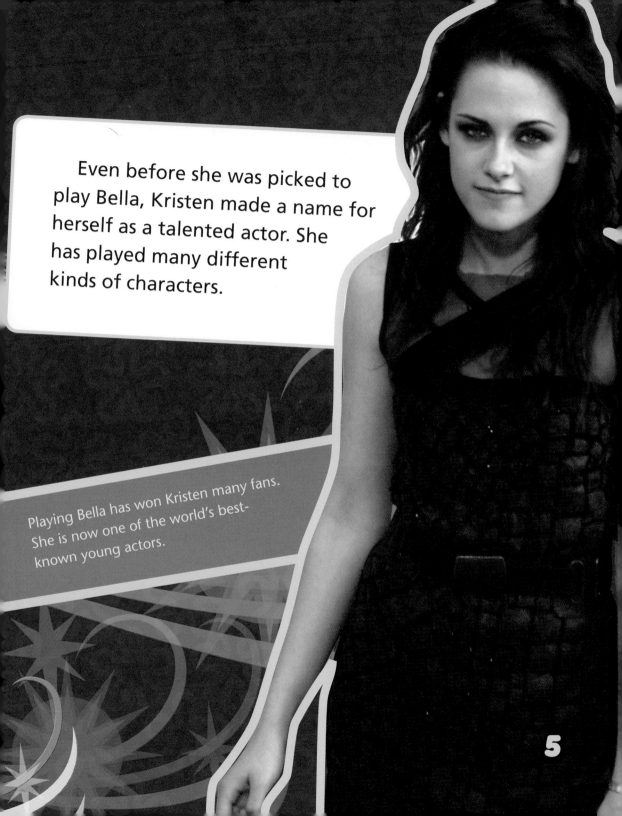

Even before she was picked to play Bella, Kristen made a name for herself as a talented actor. She has played many different kinds of characters.

Playing Bella has won Kristen many fans. She is now one of the world's best-known young actors.

5

Kristen was born on April 9, 1990, in Los Angeles, California. Kristen's parents are Jules Mann-Stewart and John Stewart. She has an older brother named Cameron.

When she was eight years old, an **agent** saw Kristen sing in a school show and suggested she take up acting. In 2001,

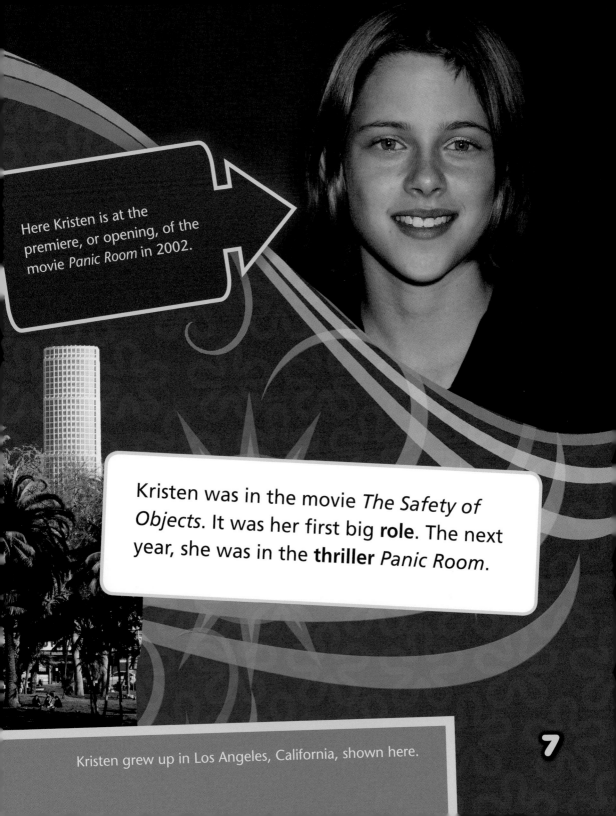

Here Kristen is at the premiere, or opening, of the movie *Panic Room* in 2002.

Kristen was in the movie *The Safety of Objects*. It was her first big **role**. The next year, she was in the **thriller** *Panic Room*.

Kristen grew up in Los Angeles, California, shown here.

Over the next few years, Kristen acted in several movies. She was in scary thrillers, such as *Cold Creek Manor*, *Undertow*, and *The Messengers*. She also was in some fun adventure movies, such as *Zathura* and *Catch That Kid*.

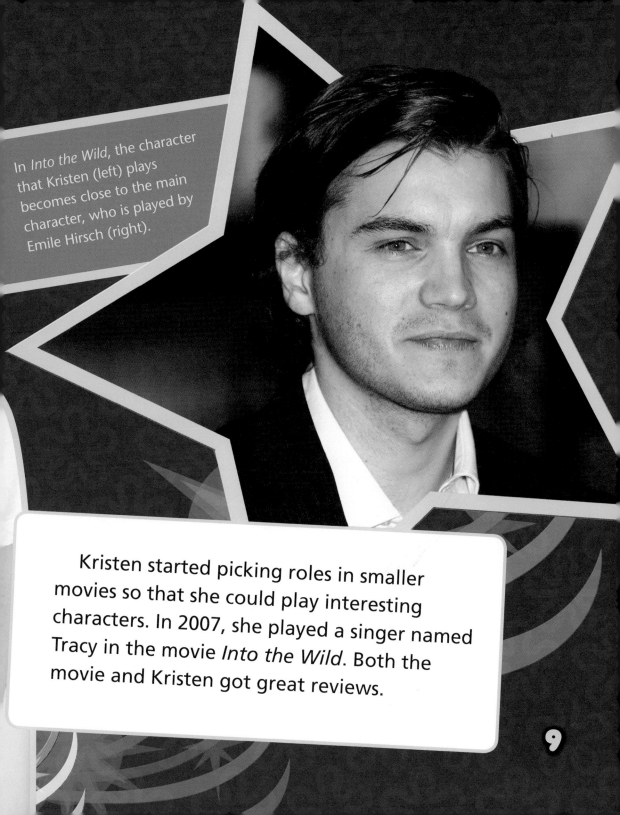

In *Into the Wild*, the character that Kristen (left) plays becomes close to the main character, who is played by Emile Hirsch (right).

Kristen started picking roles in smaller movies so that she could play interesting characters. In 2007, she played a singer named Tracy in the movie *Into the Wild*. Both the movie and Kristen got great reviews.

In 2007, Kristen was picked to play Bella in *Twilight*. In the movie, Bella falls in love with the vampire Edward Cullen. He must fight his own nature and other vampires to keep her safe.

The movie *Twilight* was based on the first book in the Twilight series. The books had

Edward Cullen is played by the actor Robert Pattinson (left). He and Kristen (right) became close while making the movie.

many fans, many of whom felt close to Bella. The people making the movie wanted to find the perfect person to play Bella. Finally, they found Kristen!

11

The Twilight Saga

In 2008, the movie *Twilight* came out. It was a huge hit. The people who made it decided to make movies out of the rest of the books in the series. In 2009, the second movie came out. It was called *The Twilight **Saga**: New Moon*.

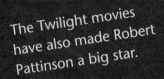

The Twilight movies have also made Robert Pattinson a big star.

Once again, Kristen Stewart and Robert Pattinson starred in the movie. Taylor Lautner, who plays Bella's friend Jacob Black, took on a starring role in this movie, too.

Kristen (middle) and her costars, Taylor Lautner (left) and Robert Pattinson (right), spoke at the MTV Video Music Awards in September 2009.

Fans Everywhere

Since the Twilight movies have been big hits, Kristen has become famous. She was surprised at how famous the movies made her. Today, fans spot Kristen when she walks down the street. They ask for her **autograph** and are curious to know everything about her.

Here, Kristen is signing autographs for fans in Westwood, California, at the premiere of *New Moon* in November 2009.

While Kristen likes meeting with fans, she does not always like all the attention she gets from reporters. She likes being an actor more than she likes being a **celebrity**.

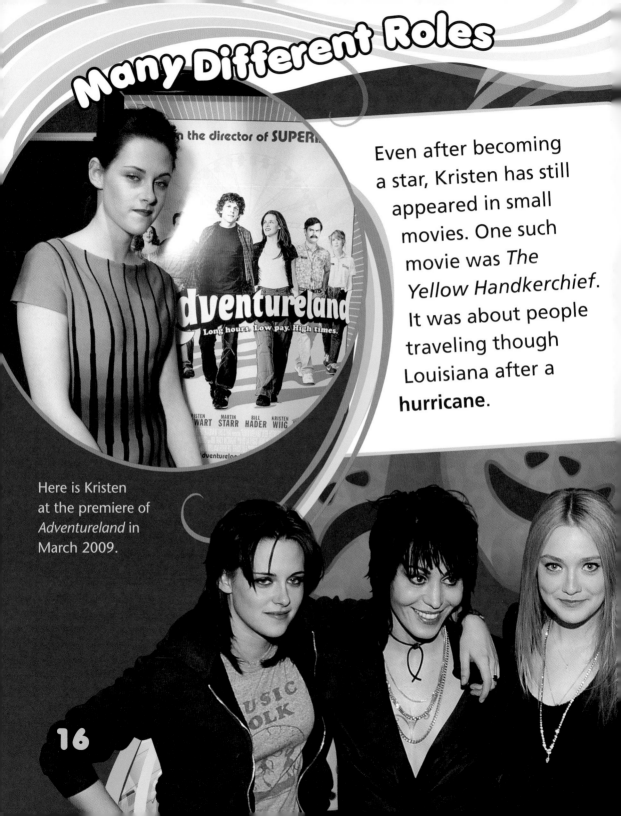

Even after becoming a star, Kristen has still appeared in small movies. One such movie was *The Yellow Handkerchief*. It was about people traveling though Louisiana after a **hurricane**.

Here is Kristen at the premiere of *Adventureland* in March 2009.

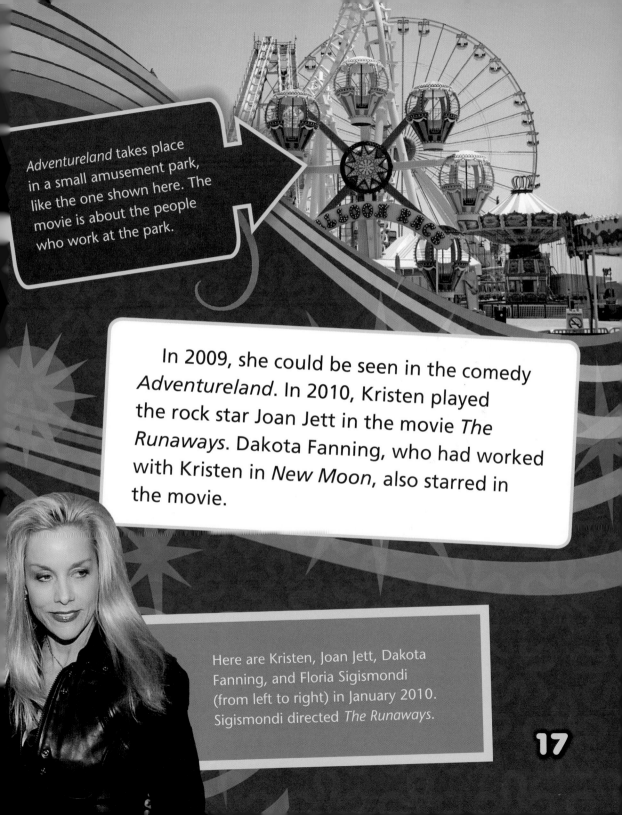

Adventureland takes place in a small amusement park, like the one shown here. The movie is about the people who work at the park.

In 2009, she could be seen in the comedy *Adventureland*. In 2010, Kristen played the rock star Joan Jett in the movie *The Runaways*. Dakota Fanning, who had worked with Kristen in *New Moon*, also starred in the movie.

Here are Kristen, Joan Jett, Dakota Fanning, and Floria Sigismondi (from left to right) in January 2010. Sigismondi directed *The Runaways*.

Kristen's Other Interests

Though she loves acting, Kristen is interested in other things, too. She has said that she would like to be a writer someday. She also likes music. She sings and plays the guitar. She likes listening to music, too. She picked the song that Bella and Edward danced to at the prom in *Twilight*.

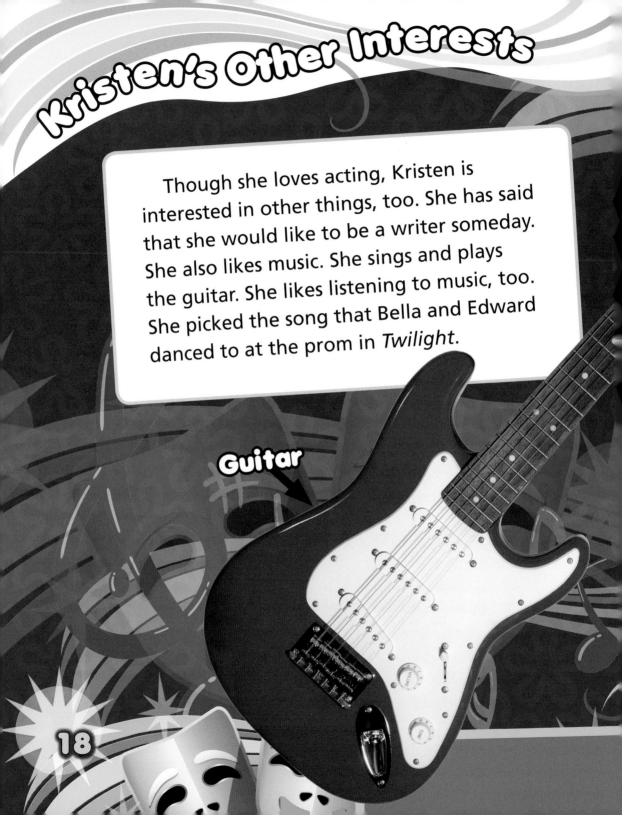

Guitar

On November 8, 2009, Kristen spoke at the Juvenile Diabetes Research Foundation's Walk to Cure Diabetes.

Kristen also works for good causes. In 2009, she took part in the Walk to Cure **Diabetes** in Los Angeles.

Kristen got to play guitar when she played Joan Jett in *The Runaways*.

In 2010, *The Twilight Saga: Eclipse* came out. In this third Twilight movie, Bella has to deal with more danger. She also must choose between Jacob and Edward forever.

In the **future**, Kristen plans to star in *Breaking Dawn*, based on the fourth Twilight book. It is such a long book, it may become two movies.

Kristen has brought lots of interesting characters to life. Her fans can likely look forward to seeing plenty more in the future.

Kristen will still act in smaller movies, too. It looks like the future holds great things for her!

21

Just Like Me!

1 Kristen is known for speaking her mind. She generally dresses the way she wants, not the way other people think she should.

2 Kristen's mother is from Australia. Kristen has said that she would like to spend more time there.

3 Robert Pattinson has said that Kristen is better at sports than he is.

4 Kristen likes animals. She has had several pets, including a number of dogs.

5 Kristen likes traveling and surfing. She also likes to write.

Glossary

agent (AY-jent) A person who helps a writer, actor, or sports player with his or her job.

autograph (AH-toh-graf) A person's name, written by that person.

celebrity (seh-LEH-breh-tee) A famous person.

diabetes (dy-uh-BEE-teez) A sickness in which a person's body cannot take in sugar and starch normally.

future (FYOO-chur) The time that is coming.

hurricane (HUR-ih-kayn) A storm with strong winds and heavy rain.

role (ROHL) A part played by a person in a movie, TV show, or play.

saga (SAW-guh) A group of stories that have ties to each other.

series (SIR-eez) A group of similar things that come one after another.

thriller (THRIL-er) A movie or story that pulls you in and is scary.

vampire (VAM-pyr) A dead person from stories and folktales who sucks the blood of living people.

Index

Read More

Hurley, Jo. *Kristen Stewart: Bella of the Ball!* New York: Scholastic, 2009.

Orr, Tamra. *Kristen Stewart.* Blue Banner Biographies. Hockessin, DE: Mitchell Lane Publishers, 2009.

Vaz, Mark Cotta. *Twilight: The Complete Illustrated Movie Companion.* New York: Little, Brown, 2008.

Web Sites

For Web resources related to the subject of this book, go to: www.windmillbooks.com/weblinks and select this book's title.